I have facilitated grief recovery su[...] ducted numerous seminars on "Re[...] ilies." As a hospital chaplain, I have counseled and comforted thousands of family members before and after the death of a loved one. Most significantly, I have experienced the death of my own son. This practical book, *Good-bye for Now*, provides valuable insights to help people understand their grief. It also gives sensible advice to help guide emotionally wounded people in working through their grief toward healing. In addition, it offers people solid spiritual hope to sustain and support them during times of emotional turmoil. Welby O'Brien has written a winner.

Jeffrey R. Funk, executive director
Hospital Chaplains' Ministry of America

It was my privilege to shepherd the O'Brien family through their long good-bye. Welby O'Brien knows well the territory of which she writes and provides a valuable tool for loved ones walking through the valley.

Dr. Roger Martin, pastor
Ph.D. from Dallas Theological Seminary

Pastors and churches would be wise to give this book to each person in their congregations and communities who experiences the death of a loved one. The comprehensive lists of things that need doing immediately after the loss, and also those that need to be done weeks and months later, are valuable at such a vulnerable time.

Linda Moore, GriefShare consultant
Church Initiative

Practical Help and Personal Hope
for Those Who Grieve

Welby O'Brien

CHRISTIAN PUBLICATIONS, INC.
CAMP HILL, PENNSYLVANIA

CHRISTIAN PUBLICATIONS, INC.

3825 Hartzdale Drive, Camp Hill, PA 17011
www.christianpublications.com

Faithful, biblical publishing since 1883

Good-bye for Now
ISBN: 0-87509-986-6
LOC Control Number: 2003-113775
© 2004 by Welby O'Brien
All rights reserved
Printed in the United States of America

05   06   07   08   5   4   3

DEDICATION

With thanks to the LORD for His love and grace,
and for Dad, Mom, Bobby and Kevin.

Contents

Acknowledgments

A very special thank-you to all who shared their hearts and provided both personal and professional input. I am especially grateful to Chaplain Barry Black (U.S. Senate), Pat Robertson (Christian Broadcasting Network), Dr. Tim Clinton (American Association of Christian Counselors), Linda Moore (GriefShare), Terry L. Thompson (Attorney at Law), Chaplain Jeffrey R. Funk (Hospital Chaplains' Ministry of America) and Dr. Steve Stephens for their contributions. A personal note of thanks to Pastor Roger Martin, Dianne Collard, Betty Richards, Beverly Schulz, Tom Downing, Betty White, Emily King and Mike Richardson. A sisterly word of appreciation to Bobby, who has so lovingly and capably stepped up to the plate in Dad's absence. A motherly word of thanks to Kevin for his support and understanding during these difficult days. And I could never say enough to Mom, who is victoriously living through her loss in the strength of her loving and mighty Lord.

How *to* Use *This* Book

Because everyone who reads this book comes with a unique set of circumstances and needs, there is no one right way to proceed.

The best way to begin is to understand how *Good-bye for Now* is arranged. Then you can decide where you need to start and where to go from there.

The Introduction is a brief, personal account of my own story. The rest of the book is about you. Journal pages have been included throughout the book for you to use as you desire. These pages are for your personal use, whether thoughts and feelings, reflections, memories or practical things to do.

Part One, *The Practical: Looking Outward,* is a checklist of things to do. Most of the tasks are those which require immediate attention following the death of a loved one. It is a good place to start if your loss is imminent or recent.

Part Two, *The Personal: Looking Inward,* is about taking care of you. Beginning with basic survival, you will go on to receive practical words of encouragement for healing and growth.

Part Three, *The Promises: Looking Upward,* is about the reality of our hope in God. You can find the specific promises you need to help carry you through these seemingly impossible days.

The appendices provide extra information you may find helpful as you face your grief.

You may want to start at the beginning and read straight through. Or, you might find yourself jumping around as your needs vary from day to day. You may also want to mark certain sections to read again later.

However you choose to go about it, my prayer is that you will find all you need in the eternal grace, power and presence of our loving Lord.

Introduction

Chances are you are reading this now because someone very special to you has died. It's OK if these words blur up. My own eyes also sting with tears.

Saying good-bye is never easy. It hurts like crazy. Normally when we bid our loved ones farewell, we hope to see them again. But not this time. This separation is permanent. We soon realize that we will *never* again see our loved ones. *Or will we?*

My father and I were very close. Although far from perfect, he was my dad, and I loved him. After a long, extremely difficult illness, he finally went to be with the Lord.

Knowing in your head that someone is going to die, as we *all* will, somehow doesn't adequately prepare you for the moment you receive the news. For me, it was a message on the telephone. I hung up and stood there stunned.

Immediately I was consumed with three emotions.

First I felt *intense grief and sadness.* Dad was gone. I would never again get to run up to him, embraced by his loving arms. We would never again talk on the telephone. I would never again see his smile, give him a haircut, ride horses with him or ask his advice.

Grief soon gave way to a burst of *indescribable joy!* As if he could hear me, I cheered, "Bravo, Dad! You made it! Way to go, Dad!" It was as if I could see him safely in the arms of Jesus, at peace and pain-free, the heavens rejoicing in his homecoming.

Instantly emanating from the depths of my being sprang a flood of *overwhelming gratitude!* I cried out, "Thank You, Jesus, for the cross! Thank You, Jesus!"

At that moment it all made sense. I had never been close enough to death to truly comprehend the magnitude and significance of why Christ died on the cross and rose again. At that moment, if there had been no cross and no resurrection, there would be no hope. At that moment, *nothing else mattered* for Dad except that he knew Jesus and was part of God's family forever.

For Dad, it did not matter that he was a good father or husband. At that moment and for eternity, all that mattered was that he had a relationship with his heavenly Father through Jesus Christ. Thank You, Jesus, for the cross!

Death is *not* the end. Our good-bye is only temporary. When we know Christ as our Savior, death is but a doorway into the glory of eternity with God. It is release from these corruptible earthly bodies to a place of freedom, rest and joy.

We must say good-bye for now, but we do so in eager anticipation of the most spectacular family reunion of all time, when we will be home at last, together with our Lord forever. And there we will never again say *good-bye*.

PART ONE

The Practical

Looking *Outward*

Wouldn't it be nice if we could take time off to grieve? What if we could simply go on a long vacation? Only when we were healed would we come back to face the barrage of practical matters. But the reality is that you find time to cry in between the phone calls and in the middle of sorting through files. This section will help you tackle the overwhelming number of things that need to be done in the midst of grief. It contains a fairly comprehensive list to guide you in the process.

Although every situation is unique, the tasks that need to be done are fairly universal. This list is organized from the most to the least urgent. You may want to check things off as they are completed.

RULE #1: Do only what is *absolutely essential* right now. Take care of yourself and do only what *must* be done. There will be time later for the rest.

Calls *for* Help

The very first thing you need is people by your side. Some will think for you. Others will do things you can't

Looking *Outward*

right now. Still others will just be there to comfort you. Reach out for their help, and then *let them help.* You know whom you really want with you now. Call him or her.

___ Pastor, minister or chaplain
___ Closest family members
___ Closest friend
___ Funeral director
___ Find someone to answer the phone and door and to keep records of who drops by or calls. Or you may wish not to answer the door and to make use of your answering machine.
___ In some cases, you may want to appoint someone to be the family spokesperson.
___ Ask someone to coordinate meal preparation for the week.

Releasing *the* Body

Hopefully these decisions were made prior to death. If not, the hospital, funeral home or your attorney may need to be consulted. In some states, the law requires that the funeral director be contacted immediately. He or she will take care of many of the details listed in this section. Be sure to consult with him or her to know specifically what he or she will do and what you need to be responsible for yourself.

___ See if the body was designated for donation to medical research. Locate the appropriate documents and make arrangements for release and transportation.
___ Contact the funeral home and/or make burial or cremation arrangements. Consider your budget before committing to funeral and burial expenses. It is *not* necessary to purchase the premiere package. Simple and affordable will honor your loved one just as much. (How would *he*

Looking Outward

or she want you to spend your money at this time?) Generally speaking, traditional burial is fairly close in price to that of cremation. Most funeral homes have many options for both. Caskets begin at about $400 and can cost as much as $20,000. Other burial containers are similarly priced. Costs for services, facilities, transportation and goods will be provided by your funeral home director. The most commonly chosen price range is about $2,500-$4,000.

Getting *Organized*

You'll be glad you made the effort now to get organized. With so much confusion at this time, it is tempting just to toss pertinent information on the desk or kitchen counter. Unfortunately, things can get misplaced or accidently tossed out, so that isn't a good idea. Setting up a system will help tremendously as questions arise and information is needed. Keep everything in the same place, such as a big box or a file drawer. Gather file folders, notebooks, paper and pens, and have separate file folders or notebook pages for each of the following categories and any others that you come up with yourself.

Vital statistics. You will need this information for a number of things, the most immediate being the death certificate. Although the requested information varies slightly from state to state, the following will be helpful for completion of the death certificate: full legal name, date of birth, date of death, race, state of birth, parents' names and their states of birth, social security number, most recent address, length of time in that county, education, occupation/industry, military (branch, rank, experience and discharge information), place of death, final resting place. They will also want to know how

Looking Outward

Looking *Outward*

many certified copies of the death certificate you will need. (They usually cost about $14-$17 each. Some people start with five and order more later if needed.) Finally, they will want to know where and to whom to send the certificates.

___ Notify the bank of your loved one's death and check his or her safety deposit box for important documents. You will need to be a cosigner on the box. If you are not, bring the key and a copy of the death certificate. If your name is not on the safety deposit box, the bank will only allow you to retrieve the will. You may need to consult your attorney on this matter.

___ Names of people to contact.

___ List of things you need help with when asked, "Is there anything I can do to help?"

___ Funeral/service ideas. (See "Planning the Service" later in this chapter.)

___ Financial and legal matters. (Examples: hospital/medical, vehicles, bills to pay, receipts, attorney, life insurance, bank, etc.)

___ Things to do and questions to be answered.

___ List of people to thank later.

___ Bills, mail and/or other personal items of the deceased that need to be handled.

___ Other thoughts or notes.

Notifications

As best you can, think through whom you need to contact about your loved one's death and what you want him or her to know. This can be very hard, especially if the death was unexpected. Write down whom you want to contact and what to tell each one. You may feel comfortable sharing added details with some people and not with others.

Looking Outward

Looking *Outward*

If time permits and if appropriate, you might want to consider sending written notifications. You can also ask someone else to make many of these contacts for you. There is space on the opposite page to write in the name of the person who will help you in each area.

___ Decide whether or not you want flowers (you will receive many at home and at the service unless you request no flowers). If there are allergies in the family or if you just prefer that donations go elsewhere, you can simply state "no flowers, please."

___ Do you wish to designate any specific charities for donations in memory of the deceased?

___ Talk with the funeral director to set the date, time and location for the viewing and/or funeral and/or memorial service and/or graveside service. Find out specifically what the funeral home will be responsible for and what you need to do (several of the items on this list will be taken care of by the funeral director).

___ Write out the obituary. (See your local newspaper or Appendix A at the back of this book for samples.)

___ Decide if you want the responsibility of housing visiting guests or if it would be wiser to assist them in finding suitable lodging nearby.

___ Notify friends, coworkers, military personnel and relatives of the loved one's death. Keep in mind that the people in your life may not all be the same people who were part of your loved one's life. Be sure to notify those who knew your loved one as well as those who may just know you and want to be there to support you.

___ Contact newspapers in areas you wish to place the funeral notice and/or obituary. (See appendix A for sample funeral notices and a sample obituary.)

___ Notify your church and that of the deceased.

Looking Outward

Looking Outward

___ Notify your place of employment and request some time off.

___ If the deceased was employed, notify his or her boss and coworkers.

___ If the deceased lived alone, notify his or her landlord and utility companies.

Planning *the* Service

Some people have the awkward blessing of being able to plan their own services while they are still living. They may discuss with loved ones what they want or leave their wishes in written form. If they have not, those who are left must do their best to plan a service that would both please the one who is gone and at the same time fulfill their own needs and desires.

Some people opt not to have a service. For any number of reasons, they just may not want one. Unfortunately, many look back later with regret. The benefits of a funeral or memorial service far outweigh any cost, pain or inconvenience. It provides an outlet for the emotional needs of grief and mourning. The reality and finality of the loved one's death helps the griever move toward closure. It can be a ceremony, such as a rite of passage, or a celebration that the loved one has gone ahead to be with the Lord. It is a time to commemorate the life that has been lived. Family and friends have the opportunity to pay tribute to the one who influenced their lives. Those in mourning are surrounded with the love and support they so desperately need. And it forces us all to pause. We cannot help but reflect on what is truly important in this life.

A sample service order is provided in Appendix B. Use the following checklist to help you organize your thoughts.

Looking Outward

Looking *Outward*

___ Write down what *you* want and what you remember your loved one wanted.

___ Discuss your thoughts about the service with family members.

___ If there is a viewing, decide if it is appropriate for young family members to participate.

___ Write down everything you want the minister to know and/or say about the life and memories of your loved one.

___ Meet with your minister (or whoever will be officiating) to plan the following:

○ Confirm the date, time and location.

○ Decide on the music and musicians: instrumentalists, soloist/vocal group, congregational singing, prelude/postlude, music for the reception. Will you personally contact these people, or will you ask someone else to do it? (If you would like to have someone else do it for you, make a note of his or her name and phone number and contact him or her as soon as you can so that he or she has time to get the necessary things done.) Is there any kind of prerecorded music you want to use?

○ Select ushers, casket bearers (usually six), food servers and any other people needed to help. Will you personally contact them, or will you ask someone else to do it? Again, if you would like to have someone else do it for you, make a note of his or her name and phone number and contact him or her as soon as you can so that he or she has time to get the necessary things done.

○ Choose what Scriptures you want to include.

○ Include any poetry special to you or your loved one.

Looking Outward

Looking *Outward*

○ Draft the written program or memorial to distribute. Who will be responsible to type, print and deliver it to the service?

○ Go over your notes (and suggestions from other family members and friends) about the life and special memories that you want shared.

○ Will there be a ceremony or special recognition for his or her military enlistment, endeavors and/or achievements?

○ Do you want open sharing or designated testimonials?

○ Plan the food: Who will buy it, fix it, serve it and clean up afterward?

○ Do you want to buy flowers? Unless you specify otherwise, people will likely have them sent to the service. You need to decide what you want done with them following the service (donate to church, nursing home, etc.).

○ Will you want a photo of your loved one displayed in front or at the entrance? Locate the picture(s) you wish to include and designate someone to enlarge, frame, display and return them. Video presentations and photo collages are becoming more common in services. Have a friend locate a professional who can help you with this if you are interested.

○ Consider displaying any special mementos, such as a doll, craft, hat, baseball, book, figurine, etc.

○ Arrange for someone to purchase a guest registry book for guests to sign as they come in. Be sure to have that person give it to you later.

○ In the entry area, you may want to include paper, pens and a box for people to write short notes to

Looking Outward

Looking *Outward*

you. You will appreciate reading them later when things quiet down.

○ Decide (with other family members if appropriate) what will be on the headstone.

Chaplain Jeffrey R. Funk, executive director of Hospital Chaplains' Ministry of America, officiates at an average of eighty funerals every year. He has compiled the following list of questions which he has found very helpful in preparing for a memorial, tribute or eulogy. You may wish to ponder these on your own or go over them with the officiating minister.

○ What adjectives and/or adverbs would you use to best describe his/her character?

○ Where was he/she born? Where did he/she grow up? . . . go to school? How did that background influence him/her?

○ How did he/she see or describe himself/herself?

○ When you picture him/her in your memories, where do you see him/her and what is he/she doing?

○ Are there any achievements or accomplishments that he/she was proud of? That you are especially proud of? In your opinion, what was his/her greatest accomplishment?

○ Was he/she a member of any professional organization, community service club, lodge or social group? How active was he/she in this group? Did he/she receive any special recognition awards while serving in this group?

○ What was his/her primary occupation? How long was he/she involved in this career? What other types of work was he/she involved in? Did he/she

Looking Outward

Looking *Outward*

like the work? What important contributions did he/she make to his/her job?

O What are the important lessons, principles and/or values that he/she has taught you? What impact for good has he/she had upon your life and the lives of others?

O Did he/she have any particular hobbies or activities that he/she regularly pursued? Did he/she have any special talents or gifts?

O What was his/her favorite music? Did he/she have any favorite songs or hymns?

O Did he/she have any favorite poems or writers?

O Did he/she have a favorite Scripture verse or Bible story? Did he/she ever underline in his/her Bible?

O Was he/she active in a local church? How and when was he/she involved?

O How would you describe his/her spiritual journey? How would he/she want to be remembered concerning his/her faith? Did he/she consider himself/herself a Christian? Why or why not?

O Did he/she ever discuss his/her thoughts and feelings about death? Did he/she believe in life after death?

O Was there any particular cause or movement that he/she felt deeply about and strongly supported (or opposed) with time and/or money?

O Are there any special phrases or clichés that he/she used (consciously or unconsciously) that were characteristic of him/her?

O Did he/she have a nickname? Did he/she know the meaning of his/her name? How did he/she live up to that meaning?

Looking Outward

Looking *Outward*

○ What is your favorite memory about him/her? What is the funniest story you remember about him/her?

○ If he/she could have written his/her own eulogy, what do you think he/she would have included? What do you want to be sure to include?

○ If he/she had the opportunity to give you one last piece of advice, one final word of exhortation to everyone gathered at the funeral, what do you think he/she would say?

○ Because he/she has lived, how is the world he/she touched a better place?

Financial *Matters*

This part is just plain no fun. But these are things that *do* have to be done. If you are organized before you start, things will go much smoother. You may want to tackle it on your own, or you may wish to enlist the help of your favorite left-brained friend or family member.

At the very least, have *one* place to keep financial records and information. Money-related items will continue to trickle in for a long time. Just tackle the urgent things for now. Some tasks can be put off until later. (Just be aware of time-related penalties.)

___ Cancel or change names on credit cards as necessary.

___ Pay current bills:

○ Check for any payments due on debts.

○ Pay rent or mortgage. If you are cancelling the mortgage, you will need the loan number and an original copy of the death certificate.

○ Be sure insurance policies are paid up (homeowner's, personal property, casualty, life, etc.).

Looking Outward

○ Pay any outstanding real estate taxes.

___ Change names on all bank accounts if appropriate.

___ Update Social Security (1-800-772-1213):

○ Notify S.S. of the recipient's death and inquire about lump sum death benefit (for burial expenses).

○ Refund payments made after the date of death.

○ Ask your attorney if you should file form SS-4 (trust identification number).

○ Apply for widow's/widower's benefits or benefits for children under age eighteen.

___ Notify Medicaid of the recipient's death. You can reach them at Medicare (1-800-633-4227).

___ Contact insurance companies:

○ Locate insurance policies and annuities (life, health, work, auto, medical, union, credit accounts, G.I., etc.).

○ Call life insurance companies and send death certificates. If you are unsure about life insurance, call the Policy Search Department of the American Council of Life Insurance at 1-202-624-2000.

○ If there is G.I. insurance, call 1-800-669-8477.

○ If applicable, call the Veterans' Administration for the $150 cemetery allowance (1-800-827-1000), or get Form DD214 for burial and other benefits.

___ Prepare for taxes:

○ Meet with an accountant or financial advisor.

○ Make an accurate record of last illness expenses and burial costs for deduction on 1040 (or Form 706 Federal Estate Tax Return).

○ Locate tax returns for the last five years.

Looking Outward

Looking Outward

○ Review income tax returns for the last five years for tax loss carry forward.

○ File form 1041 U.S. income tax return for Estates and Trusts for the balance of the year (only required for trusts, not wills).

○ File form 1040 U.S. individual income tax return for the balance of the year (use a joint return if appropriate).

○ Determine if form 706 U.S. estate (and GST) tax return needs to be filed.

○ Call IRS for any other questions (1-800-829-1040).

___ Contact the human resource department of former employer(s) for any pensions or other benefits.

___ Collect debts owed.

___ If there are creditors, file "notice to creditors" form with the county clerk and publish it in a local newspaper. (Check individual state laws; usually this must be done within six weeks of the date of death.)

___ For stockholders, contact your local broker.

___ Check with your financial advisor before you roll over an IRA.

Special note: Some of these telephone numbers may change after the date of this publication. For current information, check the Internet or the government pages of your phone book.

Legal Matters

Unless your situation is uniquely simple, you may find it well worth your while to hire an attorney. The more responsibility you can roll over onto others, especially things outside your area of expertise, the better. Also, family disputes are less likely with a neutral third party at the helm.

Looking Outward

Looking *Outward*

Attorneys are very expensive, but in many cases well worth it. In the long run they might even save you money! It is also important for your own peace of mind to know that your legal matters are in capable hands.

As you proceed with this section, don't be intimidated by unfamiliar terms. Some of this may not make a lot of sense to those of us who are not lawyer types. Your attorney will know the language.

___ Order death certificates (you may need anywhere from five to twenty, depending on transactions) either through the mortuary where the service is held or the health department of the county in which the death occurred. Certified copies will be needed for many things.

___ Locate will and trust documents.

___ Contact executor.

___ Contact attorney.

The first thing your attorney will want to know is whether the deceased had prepared a will or a living trust. He or she will want to determine whether or not the estate needs to go through probate court. Probate is a legal process in which the court makes sure that all the debts of the deceased are paid and the assets are distributed according to the will. If there is no will, the court will distribute the assets according to state law. The probate process can take time, usually from nine months to two years before the assets can be distributed to the heirs.

If the deceased had a living trust, you can avoid the long probate process, provided that the title to all the assets was held inside the trust. Ask for assistance with the following as applicable:

Looking Outward

- Identify the trustees.
- Check the trustees' powers.
- Identify the sub-trusts.
- Establish the certification of trust.
- Prepare an affidavit of surviving trustee.
- Review for any special allocation and distribution of personal effects.
- Identify the beneficiaries.
- Check that all assets are in the living trust. (If not, the pour-over will must be probated.)

If the deceased had a will, ask for assistance with the following as applicable:

- Identify the executor.
- Identify the beneficiaries.
- Review for any special allocation and distribution of personal effects.
- Check to see how the title to the property is held. (If it is in joint tenancy, probate can be delayed until the surviving spouse dies.)

___ Locate important papers:

- Vehicle titles
- Veteran's papers, including copy of discharge
- Marriage certificate (if applicable; needed for Social Security Administration)

___ Go to the Department of Motor Vehicles. Take an original copy of the death certificate and transfer the title to the vehicles.

___ Summarize assets:

- List all assets and the title to each.

Looking *Outward*

- Value all assets as of the date of death (if required by terms of the trust or will).
- Get a written valuation of real estate (if required by terms of the trust or will; you may need an appraiser).
- Transfer the title of assets to heirs as appropriate.

Caring for Those Who Are Left

In many situations, the one who passed away had previously been the primary caregiver for someone else. Those who depended on that individual could be a spouse, child, elderly parent, friend or family member, handicapped person, invalid, roommate or pet. If the dependent person is not you, it may be up to you to be sure the dependents are cared for. The most urgent need would be to provide temporary care now and then make arrangements for the long term.

___ Arrange for temporary care of the individual(s) who were dependent on the deceased.

___ Decide who is ultimately responsible for the individual(s) and ask this party to look into options for long-term care.

___ If you are able to be responsible for the dependent person, take the necessary steps to do so. However, in most cases, the caregiver will not be you. If it is not you, get a commitment from the person who will ultimately be responsible and agree on a date when he or she will take over. In the meantime, have that person look into all the options for long-term care to discuss with you.

___ Arrange for the temporary care of pets.

___ Ask someone to be responsible for the permanent care of pets.

Looking Outward

Looking *Outward*

Dispersing *Belongings*

This is a very difficult and painful task. Many decisions have to be made at a time when you can barely function, let alone make coherent judgments. Dealing with a loved one's belongings is like having him or her there with you as you sort through many memories; yet with each item comes the stark realization that he or she is *not* there, nor will he or she ever be again. Use this as an opportunity to heal through grieving. Enjoy the memories. Let yourself cry. And let yourself laugh.

___ Immediate needs:
- First get rid of the things that need to be discarded, such as food, medications, trash, etc.
- Wash bedding.
- Wash and put away any dirty clothes.

___ Property:
- Consult the executor of the will to determine who is to receive what.
- Get a real estate agent if necessary.

___ Clothes and personal items:
- Decide with other family members where the clothing will go (family, friends, specific charities, etc.). It takes some of the sting out when you know the items are going to a worthy cause, especially one your loved one would have chosen.
- Set a time to sort through the items. Do it in phases, a little at a time. For instance, plan to go through all the shoes and accessories one day, the closet another day, the dresser another day.

Looking Outward

Looking *Outward*

○ Keep a record of all donated items, their approximate value, the date donated and the benefactor charity.

___ Pictures and memorable items:

○ Sort through them, keeping all the special things.

○ Remember to set aside items for other friends and family who would treasure them.

RULE #2: *When in doubt, wait.* If you are not sure whether you are ready to give something away, wait. You are the one who decides when. Take as much time as you want—there is no hurry. You can always do it later. Better to be sure than to regret.

Responding *to* Kind *Acts*

Along with experiencing a great loss comes the realization of how much people care. The blessing of calls, cards, gifts, donations to charity and thoughtful acts of kindness will brighten your journey through this difficult valley. As you consider how to respond, keep in mind that these people are ministering to *you*. Let them. You may feel self-imposed pressure to repay them in a way other than simple thank-you notes, but don't forget that they want you to receive their love and support and are not expecting any reciprocation. In some cases that reciprocation may even be offensive to them, as they want the joy of ministering to you.

___ Thank-you notes are *not* necessary for cards and phone calls.

___ Save all your cards. You will want to read them again as time passes.

Looking Outward

Looking Outward

___ Keep a record of all flowers and other gifts you receive as well as charitable donations made in memory of your loved one. Include the date, person's name, address and gift.

___ Send a simple thank-you card to each. Keep the writing to a minimum. For example: *Thank you so much for the____. Your thoughtfulness and friendship have meant a lot to us through the years.*

___ Do only one or two notes a day as you feel up to it. There is no need to hurry, but it would be good to have them all sent within two months.

___ Verbal thank-yous are also acceptable.

Congratulations! If you've made it this far, you are doing great! Remember to be good to *yourself*. If you haven't already, be sure to take the time to read the next section. It will help you optimize your survival and complete the healing process.

Looking Outward

_____
_____
_____
_____
_____
_____
_____
_____
_____
_____
_____
_____
_____
_____
_____
_____
_____
_____
_____
_____
_____

Looking Outward

PART TWO

The Personal

Looking Inward

Taking care of yourself is probably the last thing on your list right now. You've been caught up in the whirlwind of demands that keep you in constant motion.

Remember Rule #1? *Do only what is absolutely essential right now.*

Rule #2 was *When in doubt, wait.*

Now for the next rule.

RULE #3: Take care of *you.*

Looking inward is necessary for your own health and survival as you walk through this valley of grief. In the long run, it will ultimately be crucial for your healing.

When I was grieving, I felt I still had to do all the things I had been doing in addition to all the things that now fell on my shoulders. Unfortunately, it took an emotional and physical collapse for me to realize I had to rearrange my priorities. I wish someone had said to me, "You have permission just to take care of you. Everything else can wait."

Your job right now is just to survive. Do what you can that must be done and put the rest on hold. You won't have to do it forever—only for now. Give yourself permission right now. If you don't, you may end up being no good to anybody.

Put yourself at the top of the list today and tomorrow. As you take care of *you*, you will find greater strength to meet the challenges ahead.

1. How can I survive during this overwhelming time of grief?

Through the years, I have realized that if I don't nurture myself, it's possible that no other human being will. Contrary to what many Christians believe, taking care of yourself is not selfish: It's essential. There is no inherent valor in ignoring your personal needs. In fact, only when we meet our needs in a healthy way will we be adequately equipped to minister to others.

The following is an adaptation of the Survival Checklist from *Formerly a Wife* (Horizon Books, 1996). As you go through this survival checklist, give yourself a cheer for those areas in which you are doing well. Then make a special note by those that need more attention. I also encourage you to use the space provided at the end of this chapter to write out your thoughts and feelings.

___ **Pour out your heart to God.**

There will be times when you come before Him and have no words. At other times you will have words, some more acceptable than others. He just wants you to come to Him. Let Him know you need Him. Cry out in pain. Lash out in anger. Weep before Him as you ask, *Why?*

Acknowledge who He is. Do you need a Good Shepherd? The God of all comfort? A hiding place? An all-knowing, wise Guide? A Provider? A loving Heavenly Father? An all-powerful Advocate? Once you acknowledge who He is, lay your petitions at His feet. Claim His promises. Take comfort in His eternal love.

Looking Inward

There is no one right way to pray. Just open up your being and let it all out. He is listening. Although it may be hard to understand right now, He does care for you (see 1 Peter 5:7). He knows what pain is. He knows what death is. And He hates them just as much as you do. Open your heavy heart and let Him have it as it is. He wants you. Right now. As you are.

___ **Immerse yourself in God's Word.**

God's Word is true, powerful and supernatural. And yet it is amazingly personal. We speak to Him through prayer; He speaks to us through the Bible. His Word brings strength, hope, comfort and peace. Ask Him to show you a special promise or word of encouragement today. Let Him love you. Open your heart to His comfort.

God's Word was written under inspiration by real people with real feelings. Explore the third section of this book designed specifically for those who have suffered loss. Find the verses that speak to you. Then write down these special verses to carry with you, or put them up where you will see them throughout the day.

I have found that "refrigerator verses" are a great source of encouragement. When you come across a verse that is especially meaningful, write it down and put it up on your refrigerator. That supernatural message will touch you many times, whether consciously or subconsciously.

There will be times when you want to absorb all you can, and the Bible will satiate your starving heart. At other times you will feel you don't have the strength to even pick up the book. That's OK too. He understands.

The more our minds are filled with the Lord and the reality of hope in Him, the easier it is to go on.

Looking Inward

___ **Put off major decisions for at least one year.**

The first year is the hardest. Although it does get better, it is necessary to live through all four seasons, with the special holidays, birthdays, anniversaries and other memories. Healing takes time.

Along with healing comes clearer thinking. You will be a stronger person in a year. Put off selling the house, leaving your job or giving away significant items. Circumstances will change and so will you. Because of this, it is advisable to wait before making major decisions that can be postponed.

___ **Feel the feelings in a healthy way.**

It almost does an injustice to the intensity of what you're experiencing to label the feelings. Sadness. Grief. Anger. Relief. Guilt. They sound so simple. "Just get over it—time heals all," people say. If only it were that simple!

Only you and the Lord know the deep anguish piercing your very being. At times you are consumed with anger at the injustice of your loved one's death. *It's not fair! Why?!* At other times you beat yourself up for all of the "should haves" or what you said or failed to say in those final days. Your loneliness is unbearable. Thoughts of suicide tempt you in your dark moments.

And then you feel guilty for having these feelings, and the cycle goes on.

Reassure yourself that you are *not* responsible for any feelings that come uninvited. You are only responsible for what you do with them. First, identify the feeling. Own it. Say, "I am angry!"

Beware of the temptation just to cover up the pain. As human beings, we want to feel good. We have become masters at avoiding discomfort by immediately covering it up with something that makes us feel good (eating, drinking, television, reading, spending money, hiding out on the Internet,

Looking Inward

etc.). Facing the feelings head-on will help the healing process, both in speed and in thoroughness. Stuffed feelings do not go away. They only keep building and eventually resurface in a worse way. Be very careful not to allow yourself to slip into these dangerous escapes.

After you identify a feeling, then find a healthy outlet. What can you do to release that feeling in a constructive way? The most effective outlet for you will vary, depending on the feeling, the circumstances and you. Some options to consider are crying, journaling (in private), writing (to share), talking, yelling, running, cleaning, singing, playing a musical instrument, exercising, yardwork, going for a walk, cuddling or playing with a pet, etc. Pruning bushes has been very therapeutic for me. (The neighbors can always tell how I'm doing by what's left of my shrubs!)

Learn to say ouch. It's OK to hurt. It's *necessary* to cry. It's *good* for you to grieve. The more you let the "stuff" out in a healthy way, the better you will feel and the sooner you will heal.

____ **Talk to someone trustworthy. Get support.**

Who are the people you can share with—family, friends, chaplain, pastor, counselor or someone else? Now is the time to surround yourself with good, healthy, wise, supportive individuals who really want your best.

Some may have also walked through the valley of grief. Others won't know what you are going through but will care as they provide the love, encouragement and practical help you need.

There will be times when you don't feel like talking. You are exhausted and really don't want to talk to anyone. That is OK.

Ask your pastor or counselor if there are any grief support groups around. It can be a tremendous help and comfort to share with others who are also going through grief and to benefit from their experiences. One such group is GriefShare. You can check to see if they have groups in your area: www.griefshare.org.

As awkward and uncomfortable as it may be, it is *very* important for you to talk about the one who is gone. Get into the habit of remembering and sharing little stories with those around you. Laugh. Cry. Talk.

___ Keep your sense of humor.

Humor is the farthest thing from your mind right now. You may wonder if you will ever laugh again. Even if you could, it almost seems sacrilegious. Laughing while in mourning seems to imply that you really didn't care. The more morose your countenance, the greater your grief—right?

We can bury that myth right now. Scripture has taught for centuries what medical research is just now validating: "A merry heart doeth good like a medicine" (Proverbs 17:22, KJV). Appropriate laughter is actually *good* for you, physically and emotionally.

Be careful not to use humor as avoidance for healthy grieving. However, if something funny comes up, laugh! Enjoy the release. Let yourself laugh at memories of your loved one. Laugh alone or with others who also remember. And don't be surprised if tears accompany the process. It is possible (and OK) to laugh and cry at the same time.

___ Carefully choose your sources of input.

It's especially important during this time to monitor what you take in. Books and other reading material, Internet activity, television, movies, radio, seminar tapes, music and input from people can greatly impact your well-being. It is your responsibility to choose wisely.

You may need to avoid certain things from your regular routine for a while until you can better handle them. For in-

Looking Inward

stance, in the loss of a spouse or fiancé, romantic music and movies can be devastating. In any loss, it's normal to find that movies about death that never bothered you before will disturb you greatly.

Provide yourself with as much positive input as you can. Avoid negative or disturbing sources. There may even be some people you need to eliminate from your life for now. Remember: Your goal now is to survive. Your own well-being is at the top of your priorities.

___ Make sleep a priority.

Sleep is one of the hardest things to do at first, but it is absolutely essential. *You need your sleep.* A full night's rest as well as an afternoon nap will help replenish the strength so easily spent these days. If you are having trouble, ask your doctor for something to help during this time. Sleeping pills or some form of sedative may be necessary. Avoid caffeine if at all possible. Remind yourself that sleep is our restorative companion, not a luxury. Remember Rule #3: *Take care of* you.

You'll be glad you made this a priority as you discover more strength and clearer thoughts to help you through each day.

___ Fill your body with healthy things.

A general would never send his troops into battle without adequate weapons and supplies. Similarly, your body is on a physiological battlefield right now. It is up to you to supply and reinforce it with all that is necessary to win this war. Stress weakens the immune system. Anything you can do to build up your resistance will be beneficial.

People react differently in times of stress. Some turn to food for comfort. Others are unable to eat at all. Wherever you are on the continuum, do your best to get the nutrients you need. Just knowing this isn't enough. You have to remind

Looking Inward

and encourage yourself. Make every effort to eat and drink what's good and to avoid what is not. You may want to consider giving yourself an extra boost with additional nutritional supplements.

___ **Do some physical activity every day.**

The days will fly by in a blur. You'll wonder where the time goes and how it is possible to get everything done. Exercise is usually a low priority.

Taking care of yourself requires that you find time for physical activity. Just twenty to sixty minutes a day of moving your body aerobically will actually increase your energy and help you think more clearly. Choose an activity you like. Even if you don't feel like doing it, make yourself. Once you get going, and especially when you're done, you will feel great! Exercise releases endorphins, the body's natural tranquilizer and mood enhancer. It also boosts your immune system and helps you sleep better.

___ **Let yourself feel special.**

Self-deprivation is not a virtue. During this difficult time, you have the privilege of reminding yourself that you are special. Hopefully you will be surrounded by many friends and loved ones who will nurture, support and comfort you. Let yourself accept, feel and enjoy this attention. You need it now more than ever.

You may also need to do extra things for yourself. Stop and smell the flowers in your living room. Get a massage. Relax in a hot tub. Buy a new outfit. Listen to your favorite CD.

You are special. Don't forget.

___ **Decide when to take some time off and when to be actively involved.**

Whether work, ministry or social commitments, every activity takes time and energy. Right now you are surviving,

Looking Inward

getting through each day by taking care of what *must* be done. By sundown, there isn't much left. It may be necessary to take a leave of absence from some of your activities.

Don't worry about what others may think. If they don't understand, there is something wrong with them. Most people know you need time to deal with your loss practically, physically and emotionally. Inform them that you will look forward to rejoining them again before long, and don't feel pressured to committing to a date at this time. But if you must, allow yourself at least three to six months before jumping back in 100 percent.

In some cases, your activity may actually be good for you. Ask yourself, *Is this energizing and lifting me up, or is it depleting and draining me? Is it building me up or taking away from strength I need to use elsewhere at this time?*

Looking Inward

___ **Let go of what is beyond your control.**

It is very easy to fret about the past and to worry about the future. Whatever the circumstances, there is probably someone you feel is to blame. Forgiveness for him or her, or yourself, seems impossible. You feel bombarded with all the "should haves" and "if onlys." Since your loved one's death, the future is overflowing with uncertainties. There is a lot to do, and even more you don't know how to do. The past, the present and the future are overwhelming.

Try asking yourself this question: *Have I done everything that I can do?* If not, then make a list of what you can still do. Don't think about it any more until the next day or when you are able to do what's on the list. If you have done everything you can, then consciously let go. Remind yourself that you have done all you can.

Letting go implies that what you were holding on to is now going elsewhere. What better place could it go than into the hands of God! He is the One who understands your anger, fears and confusion. Let Him vindicate where there has been an injustice. Trust Him to lead you through the uncertainties of tomorrow.

Let go and let God. *He* is able.

___ Count your blessings.

The loss of a loved one is all-consuming. Not much else fills your mind in these days of grief; therefore it is necessary to stop and consciously focus on all you *do* have. Take inventory of your blessings. You can do this alone and also with others who share your loss.

Start by thinking of the positive things that have happened recently. Perhaps you may remind yourself that your loved one is no longer in pain; perhaps you could focus on the love and support of those around you. Then look at how your needs are being met. Consider everything that we are prone to take for granted. Try to name ten things every morning or evening.

Gratefulness is a choice. Though you cannot change your circumstances, you can affect how you perceive them. Your world will brighten as you choose to give thanks even if you don't feel like it at the time.

___ Trust God.

Perhaps your faith in God has been shaken a bit lately. That is normal. You wonder, *How could He allow this? Where has He been, and why didn't He answer my prayers?*

We have to take an honest look at what Scripture says. He never promised us a comfortable life here, and we know we all have an appointment with death at some time. *He* knows that, and that is the whole reason He sent his Son to die for us on the cross.

When God knew we were helpless sinners, He could have abandoned us. Instead He came to earth to suffer and die *for*

Looking Inward

us! He triumphantly conquered death forever! His resurrection is the greatest victory in all eternity!

We cannot always count on people. The medical community is not perfect. Our law enforcement system is flawed. People make mistakes. But we can trust the One who died for us. And now alive forever, He is waiting for you with open arms. Just let Him hold you. Let Him tell you how much He loves you. Claim His promises. You can choose to trust even if you can't feel it. He is the only One worthy of your trust.

____ **Let time work.**

It will get better. As you continue to do what needs to be done and take healthy steps each day, the healing will progress. Avoid setting any time limits on your grief. You may grieve until the day you die. And that's OK. But it will get better.

You'll find that you go for longer periods of time in between bursts of grief, and the intensity of the pain will ease. Let it proceed. Don't rush. Allow yourself to grieve every time you feel that burning in your throat and stinging in your nose as you struggle to hold back the tears. Don't fight. Let it come out.

Go with the ups and downs of this unpredictable roller coaster ride for as long as it takes. You are doing great. Let time work for you. Let God work in you.

2. What are the stages of grief, and is there a prescribed way to go through them successfully?

Several misconceptions exist about grieving. Be encouraged to know that there are no rules and no best way to proceed through the different stages of grief. Everybody grieves in different ways, at different times and at different rates. Your own healing process will be unique to you.

Another fallacy is that grief is linear: a person goes through the steps and eventually "graduates." The grieving process is more like a series of cycles and is never totally complete. As you heal, you will find some areas becoming less intense and other areas recurring. The key is to work through them in a healthy way as they arise, no matter how long it takes.

The point of categorizing grief into stages is to let you know what you are experiencing is normal and necessary for your survival and healing. It is also a way to provide a general guideline so you can see if there are any major gaps in your own progress. There are many opinions on the exact names and number of phases. Generally most counseling professionals agree on the basic process. I view the phases of grief as follows:

Shock and denial

This is a subconscious survival technique to get you through the first part. You are numb. The human body and emotions can only process so much at one time. Gradually, as you become better oriented, this natural novocaine will wear off. Reality will begin to set in and you will feel.

Emotional reactions

Do not be surprised at any feeling that arises. The range is wide, intense and unpredictable. There will likely be anger, guilt, pain, relief, loneliness, anguish, bitterness and fear. Thankfulness could enter the picture. You may even be blessed with moments of joy. The important thing is to process every feeling in a healthy way. Face it. Feel it. Let it out.

Depression

This is an extended time of being at the very bottom. You are exhausted physically and emotionally. The body needs this time to regroup and rebuild its depleted stores. It is not

Looking Inward

uncommon to experience confusion, hallucinations and yearnings for the one you so loved. Feelings of despair, hopelessness and abandonment are also a normal part of this phase. You may even entertain thoughts of suicide. It is usually a good idea to talk with your pastor, counselor and possibly your medical professional during this time.

The following symptoms should receive professional help if they occur: any self-destructive thoughts or behavior; inability to sleep; significant weight loss or gain; hallucinations or delusions; panic or anxiety attacks; unusual physical pain or symptoms; hyperactivity or compulsive behavior; inability to get out of bed or be active; overuse of medications; excessive use of alcohol; use of illegal drugs.

Acceptance and recovery

Finally there comes a time when you know your loved one is really gone. Like every other aspect of healing, acceptance comes a little at a time. Gradually you will withstand the reality more often and for longer periods of time. You will feel pain less often and less intensely. Crying spells will taper. Gradually you will be able to speak of your loved one with a steady voice. His or her passing will take its rightful place in your thoughts as a fact.

You will begin to be able to function as you once did. Acceptance does not mean that you like the loss, but that you are learning to live with it as you go on to reinvest your life. Although the pain of loss will always be there, those who once grieved become freed up to learn, grow and move forward.

The following was shared by a mother whose son was murdered:

> The goal of grief recovery isn't moving on—or even "getting over it."

Looking Inward

The goal is the rebuilding of my world, embracing the memories of both his life and death. I will never cease to grieve the loss of my son, but that doesn't mean that I'm less capable of engaging in a full and joyous life. I do not have to merely survive—God promises I can thrive—but I'll never be the same.

3. How can I come to the point of being able to say "died," "death" or "dead" without choking or crying? Is it OK to just say "passed away"?

Right now those seemingly simple words are very hard to articulate. Time will help. But to better understand, we need to look at the culture surrounding us. We live in a society that sequesters the dying rather than dealing with death as a natural part of life. Nursing homes are filled with loved ones who are far removed from the core of society.

We are further insulated by the entertainment industry, resulting in a blurred line between fact and fantasy. We like shows that end with "happily ever after." If there is a death in the show, we take subconscious comfort in knowing that it was just a movie. We can then watch something else and the bad goes away. Then when real life happens, or real death, we are unprepared and caught off guard.

At a personal level, your own response to the death of your loved one seems directly related to your physical, emotional and spiritual well-being. As you take healthy steps in the grieving process (crying, praying, getting counseling, etc.), the initial phase of denial eventually transforms into acceptance.

Most people avoid saying "death," "died" and "deceased" because they sound so abrupt and final. When we are in shock and pain, we just can't say these words. We need words of comfort and hope, like "resting in peace" and "passed on." Over time, as healing progresses, you will no longer choke on

Looking Inward

the words. You'll find you can read, write and say them with only a twinge of pain.

Another factor would be where you are on your spiritual journey. Based on my personal relationship with Jesus Christ as my Savior and the grounding of my today and tomorrow on God's Word, I do not see death as an end but a beginning. Because of God's promises, I find it natural to say that my father (who also knew the Lord) "went to be with the Lord" and is "finally home." The sting is still there, but the underlying peace is unmistakable. I hope that your loved one is also with the Lord and that you will one day join him or her there.

There really is no best way to say that your loved one is gone. All the semantics and sugarcoating in the world won't bring back the one you lost. But take heart: Someone isn't lost if you know where he or she is.

4. What is the best way to help children with their grief?

In their own backyard, two little boys witnessed their mommy suffer a heart attack and die right before their eyes. The father, now a young widower, had to grieve not only for himself but also with and for his children. Another couple was devastated when their teenage son was murdered and to this day still grieve with their other two children. These parents were among those who offer the following advice:

___ Lay a spiritual foundation.

If you have not already talked openly with your children about life, death, heaven and hell, now is a good time to start. Use the Bible as the source of truth and be prepared to back up what you say with Scripture references. Too many "feel-good" fluffy lies are inoculating our children against the good news of the *truth*. Read together and write out Scripture verses of comfort and hope. We have hope because Jesus Christ died on the cross for our sins—everybody's sin—and then came alive again. All we have to do is choose to believe Him and ask Him to forgive our sins and bring us into God's family. (See Part Three for specific verses.) Now is an ideal time to help children be sure they know the Lord and have a place reserved for them in heaven.

___ Talk openly about death and heaven.

We live in a culture that shields us from the reality of death. We must grasp the reality and pass it on to our children so that they will not be so fearful of this ominous unknown. Don't tell them "she's sleeping" or "passed on," etc. They will expect their loved one to wake up or come back. Explain simply and clearly that their loved one's body is dead. That means his or her heart won't beat any more, his or her lungs won't breathe and none of his or her body parts work anymore. Remind children that these bodies are just temporary houses, like renting a motel room for a while. Every time we get hurt or get sick or don't like the way we smell, we should rejoice that we have new bodies awaiting us in heaven.

Death is not an end. It is a doorway into a new beginning of eternity. There will always be another tomorrow. And the best part is that we are forever with the Lord, our loving heavenly Father and Savior! The other good news is that we will once again be with the one who is gone for a while. Because of Jesus, death is only a temporary separation. Even though it hurts, our good-bye is only for a little while.

___ Show them how to grieve.

The best way to help your children grieve is to let them watch you. Don't be afraid to be transparent in front of them. They need to see you sob before they can know it's OK for them to cry. Help them find healthy outlets for

Looking Inward

their sadness, anger, guilt, fear and other feelings. Buy them each a journal. Show them how to write or draw in it. Talk with them openly. Reassure them that all feelings are normal, but we have to find a healthy outlet so they don't just rot inside: crying, yelling, running, talking, praying, singing, kicking a ball, drawing a picture, hugging a teddy bear.

___ **Go to counseling together or join a grief support group.**

Your minister or counselor can be a very important part of the healing process. It might be helpful to find a Christian counselor who specializes in working with children. You may also want to consider a support group for the family.

___ **Keep change to a minimum.**

The loss of this loved one has turned your children's worlds upside down. When added to their grief, changes and disruptions are overwhelming. Just as with adults, children take comfort in the familiar. Do as much as you can to maintain former routines and provide consistency in their lives. Try to put off any major changes (such as moving) as long as possible.

___ **Talk about your loved one.**

There's a kind of hush, an unspoken taboo against bringing up the subject of the dead. Let's dispel the myth by breaking the silence so future generations can be free to express their feelings and enjoy the treasured memories. Relive special times. Laugh as you recall funny moments. Honor your loved one as you give thanks for his or her godly character and influence in your family. Remind the children that remembering sometimes stings on the surface but leaves a deep warmth inside. And it's OK if it stings.

Looking Inward

___ **Include them in the process when appropriate.**

If possible, include the children from the very start in as many decisions and activities as possible. Whether selecting the color of the grave marker or the wording of the epitaph, it may help all of you in your healing to work through these things together. The last thing you want to do is quarantine your children.

___ **Don't be afraid to say, "I don't know."**

Release yourself right now from the burden of having to have all the answers. And believe me, you will be asked. There will be times, perhaps in the middle of the night, when words fail. Just love your children. Hold them close and let yourselves weep together. Allow God's everlasting arms to comfort you. Reassure them that you are there, and even more importantly, God is there.

For more help in dealing with grief in children, see Appendix C.

5. Is it true that men and women grieve differently?

Whether men or women, the truth is that no two people grieve the same. There is both grief and mourning. Technically, grief is the composite of the private thoughts and feelings about a loss you have experienced. Mourning is the outward, public expression of that grief. Among the many factors playing a part are cultural background, cultural surroundings, individual personality and emotional makeup, relationship with the deceased, status of current relationships, support network, circumstances surrounding the death, current situation of the griever and future outlook.

All people need to cry. Unfortunately, in our society boys are brought up to stifle the tears. This results in an unnatural bottling up of normal feelings which eventually rise to the

Looking Inward

surface in other (not necessarily healthy) ways. Feelings of shame and embarrassment often plague boys and men, as well as women who have been improperly raised not to cry. Vocal sobbing accompanied by a spring of free-flowing tears is essential to healing.

Each individual will discover certain triggers for feelings of grief and ultimately tears. Some find release in long drives alone, a time to think and cry and work through the feelings in solitude. Some channel their grief energy into projects such as repairs, yard work, cleaning, remodeling, redecorating or organizing. Others process their deep grief while looking at old photos and videos. Familiar sights, sounds and smells can prompt emotions. Music is a trigger for most people. Whether in the car, at church or at home, the right music can penetrate the very depth of your being, releasing feelings you didn't know were there. Songs about God, His love, His comfort and His eternal purpose can cleanse and rebuild a broken heart.

There is no formula and no timetable for grief. Regardless of age, sex or any other factor, each individual must proceed through the valley of grief at his own pace. No matter how far the healing progresses, there will always be a part of your heart that belongs to your loved one.

6. How do I respond to people's comments politely and without falling apart?

Never apologize for crying. You are in mourning and tears are a normal part of the process. "Falling apart" or "losing it" does not indicate that you are weak or a failure. It only reinforces the fact that you are a normal human being—with a heart.

As for people and their comments, fortunately most have good intentions. Most comments you receive are meant in the best way. Sometimes, however, they are not well thought out

Looking Inward

or something is distorted in the delivery. Two instances stand out in my own experience when my father died. The first was a minister who, prior to the service, attempted to comfort our family with, "You never get over it. You just learn to live with it." At church the next day, a lady came up to my mom and said with relief, "Oh, we were glad to find out it was you. At first we thought it was the other O'Brien, who is much younger."

In moments like those, no response is warranted. Don't be surprised if you are the recipient of these clumsy attempts to comfort.

On the other hand, you will be offered many comments and asked many questions. At times you will not feel like talking, but you don't want to be rude. It is important not to let people drain you of your much-needed supply of strength. Talking to people who are not particularly close to you can consume precious energy that is needed elsewhere. In such cases or other brief encounters, it may be helpful to have some prepared responses. If you're asked, "How are you doing?" you might say:

- "A little better today, thank you."
- "We always appreciate your prayers."
- "Some days are better than others."

If that seems to satisfy the questioner, you are finished. If he or she wants to go on and you don't, try diversion. Ask the person about something in his or her life, such as, "How's John's business going?" or "How are your grandkids?" Let the person talk for a minute, then close with a one-liner, such as "It was good to see you," or "Thank you for caring," or "We appreciate your prayers." Then hang up the phone or smile as you turn and walk away. You have been polite and

Looking Inward

haven't shut the well-wisher out, but you have also protected yourself in a healthy way.

Remember, you are trying to survive and heal. People should be there to give to you, not take away.

7. Is it normal to expect conflict between relatives after a death in the family?

A lot depends on how the relationships were prior to the loved one's death. The combination of grief's emotional toll and increased stress levels leaves everybody on edge. Tension is apt to be present. How each individual handles that tension will likely determine the level of conflict.

Another factor would be how prepared the family was in advance. Was the death anticipated or sudden? Did family members have a fairly good idea of how assets were to be distributed? Was it clear who would be making major decisions?

Because there are so many decisions to be made, the odds are that not everybody will be happy with everything. Likewise, when the assets are dispersed, there will likely be a few disgruntled family members.

Your mind-set as you go into all of this will play a big part in how you emerge on the other side. There are two things to consider. First, determine the value of your relationship with this person(s). Are you prepared to preserve the relationship at all costs, or is there a limit? You need to decide what will be most important to you a year from now. (Which is more important—how big the casket was or getting along with your sister? Who got the gold ring or enjoying Thanksgiving with your grandchildren?)

Secondly, take care of yourself and maintain healthy boundaries. Just because the person you are dealing with is related to you does not mean he or she is your favorite person. Don't let anyone take advantage of you. Be as polite

Looking Inward

and loving as possible, but be on guard against anyone just out for himself. Make the best choices you can and go on from there.

8. How do I keep healthy boundaries without hurting anyone?

You don't. If everyone else also had healthy boundaries, there wouldn't be a problem. Unfortunately, many people have no concept of boundaries. It is especially important for you to protect yourself during this healing process by setting limits on how far others can intrude in your life. This may mean drawing a line with those in your household, other family members, neighbors, friends, coworkers, consolers, telemarketers, etc.

Just where and how you draw that line is up to you. Pray for wisdom. Listen to the counsel of those around you. Ultimately, you know what you need, and you are responsible to meet those needs the best you can. It may be guarding your sleep at night or during a much-needed afternoon rest. It may be preserving precious time alone. You may choose to spend a day with your child or special friend. Don't always answer the phone. Learn to let it ring or turn off the ringer for a while each day. You can return messages when you feel like it. Practice saying no. It is not necessary to give a reason. Just a simple, "Thank you so much, but I am unable to at this time."

It is not your job right now to keep everybody happy. If you try, you will end up in the hospital.

Remember Rule #3: *Take care of* you.

9. Can I be prepared in advance for the things that may catch me off guard emotionally?

If you try to avoid pain by keeping your guard up, you will inhibit the healing process. Eventually the guard will wear

Looking Inward

down and you could have an emotional collapse. Don't be afraid to hurt. Learn to say ouch. It's OK. It's part of your journey toward healing.

The first year is usually the hardest, mainly because of all the "firsts" to face: the first Christmas without your loved one, the first Valentine's Day, the first time you go to church alone, etc. It helps a little just knowing these occasions will come. In some cases you have an opportunity to prepare yourself in advance, both emotionally as well as in scheduling. Try to fill the day with something positive while still allowing yourself to feel. Each passing day brings you a little closer to the other side of this valley.

Looking through greeting cards at the store can evoke deep feelings, both of past memories and present longings. You may want to avoid those sections which only sting your wounded heart. On the other hand, buying cards for other friends and loved ones can't replace that special person, but it might make you feel better as you warm the heart of someone else.

Don't be surprised by dreams of your loved one. Waking will be hard as you emerge from what you thought was reality. Remember to feel the feelings and to grieve in a healthy way.

Familiar sights, sounds, smells, feelings and tastes will catch you off guard. Anything can trigger your memories and instantly carry you back. Go with it. Feel it. Then go on.

Many other losses often accompany the death of a loved one, for which you may also have to grieve. Moving or selling a home can tear you apart. Leaving a job or church or neighborhood requires working through many emotions.

Grief is never simple. It is never welcome. It is never 100 percent complete. But it is there and it is necessary. Some day you will look back and see that it is good.

10. What kind of social changes and adjustments should I expect?

All mourners will experience changes in their family dynamics. Hopefully relatives will rally together to complete unfinished business and share ongoing responsibilities. If not, you can expect tension and resentment, ultimately eroding those relationships. In addition, new roles might be assumed. For example, if the father has died, the son may step up as the new patriarch or "man of the house." Another dynamic is the change in male/female ratios. In the loss of a sibling, birth order characteristics might shift. In any loss, there will be change. Adjustments take time, and a little love goes a long way in adapting.

Among the social adjustments that lie ahead will be attending someone else's funeral. It may be a while before you feel ready to attempt to go. Allow yourself as much time as you need. It will never be easy.

If your spouse has died, the challenges of adjustments may seem overwhelming at first. The sudden loneliness can be almost unbearable. Even when you are around others, you will feel the emptiness. Your identity is now being redefined. You are entering a different classification—widow or widower, which will be your label wherever you go. Adjusting to no longer being married takes a long time. It's normal if you never feel comfortable with that. This will affect all of your social life, whether at church, work or gatherings. You will miss doing things with other couples and will learn to be the "fifth wheel." How you proceed through these challenges will determine how you emerge and the person you become. You can choose to be bitter or you can choose to embark on your new adventure.

Consider attending new social groups alone or with a friend. Perhaps he or she knows of some people who get to-

Looking Inward

gether for activities. Maybe there is a group at your church that you could check out.

If you are a widow or widower, you may feel that you could never get married again. Your love for and loyalty to your spouse for all those years persuades you that there could never be another. On the other hand, that same love and loyalty could be convincing you that you want another relationship. Only you can make that decision. Let time be your friend. You will know.

Whether or not you choose to remarry, you might consider going out with a group or on a date. It will probably be good for you, and you might even have a good time. Dating again after all these years? Now *that's* a social adjustment! Have fun.

11. How can I look at my grief as more than something just to get through?

If you are a believer, you have an incredible number of promises to claim. (See Part Three of this book.) Just one of those is found in Romans 8:28. It says, "And we know that in all things God works for the good of those who love him, who have been called according to his purpose."

When He says "all things," He means all things. He doesn't promise that we will escape pain or always feel good. What He does say is that all our experiences will work together to produce the end result of goodness, both for us and for His glory.

Positive end results? At the moment we were suddenly thrust into this valley of grief, all we knew was pain. There was no relief in sight for this suddenly lonely journey. Now having progressed a bit, we may begin to see how some good might be possible. Some will have to look harder than others.

Consider the following and add your own:

- Deeper walk with God
- Closer family relationships

- Awareness of how much I am loved
- Greater appreciation of family and friends
- More accurate perspective of the important things in life
- Renewed commitment to my own health
- Newfound sensitivity to others' losses
- Increased desire to reach out to others
- Clearer understanding of life, death and eternity
- Stronger character: I am a survivor!

As you continue to make healthy choices and take care of yourself, you will gradually be able to reach out to others. Someday you will rejoice in the privilege of passing on the love and comfort you yourself have received.

Let God touch you with His healing love.

And one day He will touch someone else through you.

Looking Inward

Looking Inward

Looking *Inward*

Looking Inward

PART THREE

The Promises

Looking *Upward*

The following is a collection of verses that have been especially meaningful to me. I am learning that comfort is not the removal of pain, but it is knowing that everything is going to be all right. I hope you find the same comfort and encouragement in God's promises.

His *Presence* Our *Comfort*

Be strong and courageous. Do not be afraid or terrified because of them, for the LORD your God goes with you; he will never leave you nor forsake you. (Deuteronomy 31:6)

The LORD is my shepherd, I shall not be in want.
    He makes me lie down in green pastures,
he leads me beside quiet waters,
    he restores my soul.
He guides me in paths of righteousness
    for his name's sake.
Even though I walk
    through the valley of the shadow of death,
I will fear no evil,
    for you are with me;
your rod and your staff,
    they comfort me.
You prepare a table before me
    in the presence of my enemies.
You anoint my head with oil;

Looking Upward

my cup overflows.
Surely goodness and love will follow me
    all the days of my life,
and I will dwell in the house of the LORD
    forever. (Psalm 23:1-6)

Yet I am always with you;
    you hold me by my right hand.
You guide me with your counsel,
    and afterward you will take me into glory.

                  (Psalm 73:23-24)

O LORD, you have searched me
    and you know me.
You know when I sit and when I rise;
    you perceive my thoughts from afar.
You discern my going out and my lying down;
    you are familiar with all my ways.
. . . .

Where can I go from your Spirit?
    Where can I flee from your presence?
. . . .
If I rise on the wings of the dawn,
    if I settle on the far side of the sea,
even there your hand will guide me,
    your right hand will hold me fast.

           (Psalm 139:1-3, 7, 9-10)

So do not fear, for I am with you;
    do not be dismayed, for I am your God.
I will strengthen you and help you;
    I will uphold you with my righteous right hand.

                   (Isaiah 41:10)

Looking Upward

_____

_____

_____

_____

_____

_____

_____

_____

_____

_____

_____

_____

_____

_____

_____

_____

_____

_____

_____

Looking Upward

When you pass through the waters,
    I will be with you;
and when you pass through the rivers,
    they will not sweep over you.
When you walk through the fire,
    you will not be burned;
    the flames will not set you ablaze.
For I am the LORD, your God,
    the Holy One of Israel, your Savior;
I give Egypt for your ransom,
Cush and Seba in your stead. (Isaiah 43:2-3)

The LORD your God is with you,
    he is mighty to save.
He will take great delight in you,
    he will quiet you with his love,
    he will rejoice over you with singing.

(Zephaniah 3:17)

Promise *of* Salvation

Yet to all who received him, to those who believed in his name, he gave the right to become children of God. (John 1:12)

For God so loved the world that he gave his one and only Son, that whoever believes in him shall not perish but have eternal life. For God did not send his Son into the world to condemn the world, but to save the world through him. (John 3:16-17)

Whoever believes in the Son has eternal life, but whoever rejects the Son will not see life, for God's wrath remains on him. (John 3:36)

Looking Upward

78

Looking *Upward*

Jesus said to her, "I am the resurrection and the life. He who believes in me will live, even though he dies; and whoever lives and believes in me will never die. Do you believe this?" (John 11:25-26)

Jesus answered, "I am the way and the truth and the life. No one comes to the Father except through me." (John 14:6)

And everyone who calls on the name of the Lord will be saved. (Acts 2:21)

Salvation is found in no one else, for there is no other name under heaven given to men by which we must be saved. (Acts 4:12)

For the wages of sin is death, but the gift of God is eternal life in Christ Jesus our Lord. (Romans 6:23)

For it is by grace you have been saved, through faith—and this not from yourselves, it is the gift of God—not by works, so that no one can boast. (Ephesians 2:8-9)

For you died, and your life is now hidden with Christ in God. When Christ, who is your life, appears, then you also will appear with him in glory. (Colossians 3:3-4)

Since the children have flesh and blood, he too shared in their humanity so that by his death he might destroy him who holds the power of death—that is, the devil—and free those who all their lives were held in slavery by their fear of death. (Hebrews 2:14-15)

Looking Upward

Looking Upward

And this is the testimony: God has given us eternal life, and this life is in his Son. He who has the Son has life; he who does not have the Son of God does not have life. I write these things to you who believe in the name of the Son of God so that you may know that you have eternal life. (1 John 5:11-13)

We know also that the Son of God has come and has given us understanding, so that we may know him who is true. And we are in him who is true—even in his Son Jesus Christ. He is the true God and eternal life. (1 John 5:20)

Comfort *for* Those *Who* Grieve

When anxiety was great within me,
   your consolation brought joy to my soul.

                      (Psalm 94:19)

He tends his flock like a shepherd:
   He gathers the lambs in his arms
and carries them close to his heart;
   he gently leads those that have young. (Isaiah 40:11)

The sun will no more be your light by day,
   nor will the brightness of the moon shine on you,
for the LORD will be your everlasting light,
   and your God will be your glory.
Your sun will never set again,
   and your moon will wane no more;
the LORD will be your everlasting light,
   and your days of sorrow will end. (Isaiah 60:19-20)

As a mother comforts her child,
   so will I comfort you. (Isaiah 66:13)

Looking Upward

Looking *Upward*

"Do not let your hearts be troubled. Trust in God; trust also in me." (John 14:1)

Praise be to the God and Father of our Lord Jesus Christ, the Father of compassion and the God of all comfort, who comforts us in all our troubles, so that we can comfort those in any trouble with the comfort we ourselves have received from God. (2 Corinthians 1:3-4)

For we do not have a high priest who is unable to sympathize with our weaknesses, but we have one who has been tempted in every way, just as we are—yet was without sin. Let us then approach the throne of grace with confidence, so that we may receive mercy and find grace to help us in our time of need. (Hebrews 4:15-16)

Hope *for* Healing

I know that my Redeemer lives,
    and that in the end he will stand upon the earth.
And after my skin has been destroyed,
    yet in my flesh I will see God. (Job 19:25-26)

He heals the brokenhearted
    and binds up their wounds. (Psalm 147:3)

"I cried like a swift or thrush,
    I moaned like a mourning dove.
My eyes grew weak as I looked to the heavens.
    I am troubled; O Lord, come to my aid!"
But what can I say?
    He has spoken to me, and he himself has done this.
I will walk humbly all my years
    because of this anguish of my soul.
Lord, by such things men live;
    and my spirit finds life in them too.

Looking Upward

_____

_____

_____

_____

_____

_____

_____

_____

_____

_____

_____

_____

_____

_____

_____

_____

_____

_____

_____

Looking Upward

You restored me to health
    and let me live. (Isaiah 38:14-16)

The Spirit of the Sovereign LORD is on me,
    because the LORD has anointed me
    to preach good news to the poor.
He has sent me to bind up the brokenhearted,
    to proclaim freedom for the captives
    and release from darkness for the prisoners,
to proclaim the year of the LORD's favor
    and the day of vengeance of our God,
to comfort all who mourn,
    and provide for those who grieve in Zion—
to bestow on them a crown of beauty
    instead of ashes,
the oil of gladness
    instead of mourning,
and a garment of praise
    instead of a spirit of despair.
They will be called oaks of righteousness,
    a planting of the LORD
    for the display of his splendor. (Isaiah 61:1-3)

Yet this I call to mind
    and therefore I have hope:
Because of the LORD's great love we are not consumed,
    for his compassions never fail.
They are new every morning;
    great is your faithfulness.
I say to myself, "The LORD is my portion;
    therefore I will wait for him."
The LORD is good to those whose hope is in him,
    to the one who seeks him;
it is good to wait quietly
    for the salvation of the LORD. (Lamentations 3:21-26)

Looking Upward

Looking Upward

Do not gloat over me, my enemy!
　　Though I have fallen, I will rise.
Though I sit in darkness,
　　the LORD will be my light. (Micah 7:8)

I consider that our present sufferings are not worth comparing with the glory that will be revealed in us. (Romans 8:18)

We know that the whole creation has been groaning as in the pains of childbirth right up to the present time. Not only so, but we ourselves, who have the firstfruits of the Spirit, groan inwardly as we wait eagerly for our adoption as sons, the redemption of our bodies. For in this hope we were saved. But hope that is seen is no hope at all. Who hopes for what he already has? But if we hope for what we do not yet have, we wait for it patiently. (Romans 8:22-25)

Therefore we do not lose heart. Though outwardly we are wasting away, yet inwardly we are being renewed day by day. For our light and momentary troubles are achieving for us an eternal glory that far outweighs them all. So we fix our eyes not on what is seen, but on what is unseen. For what is seen is temporary, but what is unseen is eternal. (2 Corinthians 4:16-18)

For while we are in this tent, we groan and are burdened, because we do not wish to be unclothed but to be clothed with our heavenly dwelling, so that what is mortal may be swallowed up by life. (2 Corinthians 5:4)

May our Lord Jesus Christ himself and God our Father, who loved us and by his grace gave us eternal encouragement and good hope, encourage your hearts

Looking Upward

Looking *Upward*

and strengthen you in every good deed and word. (2
Thessalonians 2:16-17)

A *Safe* Place *of* Refuge

The eternal God is your refuge,
 and underneath are the everlasting arms.

(Deuteronomy 33:27)

You are my hiding place;
 you will protect me from trouble
 and surround me with songs of deliverance.

(Psalm 32:7)

How priceless is your unfailing love!
Both high and low among men
 find refuge in the shadow of your wings.
They feast on the abundance of your house;
 you give them drink from your river of delights.
For with you is the fountain of life;
 in your light we see light. (Psalm 36:7-9)

God is our refuge and strength,
 an ever-present help in trouble. (Psalm 46:1)

When I am afraid,
 I will trust in you. (Psalm 56:3)

Have mercy on me, O God, have mercy on me,
 for in you my soul takes refuge.
I will take refuge in the shadow of your wings
 until the disaster has passed. (Psalm 57:1)

Looking Upward

Looking *Upward*

Before the mountains were born
   or you brought forth the earth and the world,
   from everlasting to everlasting you are God.

(Psalm 90:2)

He who dwells in the shelter of the Most High
   will rest in the shadow of the Almighty.
I will say of the LORD, "He is my refuge and my fortress,
   my God, in whom I trust." (Psalm 91:1-2)

He who fears the LORD has a secure fortress,
   and for his children it will be a refuge.

(Proverbs 14:26)

When I saw him, I fell at his feet as though dead. Then he placed his right hand on me and said: "Do not be afraid. I am the First and the Last. I am the Living One; I was dead, and behold I am alive for ever and ever! And I hold the keys of death and Hades." (Revelation 1:17-18)

Strength in Times of Weakness

"Do not grieve, for the joy of the LORD is your strength." (Nehemiah 8:10)

I am still confident of this:
   I will see the goodness of the LORD
   in the land of the living.
Wait for the LORD;
   be strong and take heart
   and wait for the LORD. (Psalm 27:13-14)

Whom have I in heaven but you?
   And earth has nothing I desire besides you.
My flesh and my heart may fail,

Looking Upward

Looking Upward

but God is the strength of my heart
and my portion forever. (Psalm 73:25-26)

In that day you will say:

"I will praise you, O LORD.
　　Although you were angry with me,
your anger has turned away
　　and you have comforted me." (Isaiah 12:1)

Trust in the LORD forever,
　　for the LORD, the LORD, is the Rock eternal.

(Isaiah 26:4)

But those who hope in the LORD
　　will renew their strength.
They will soar on wings like eagles;
　　they will run and not grow weary,
　　they will walk and not be faint. (Isaiah 40:31)

"Where, O death, is your victory?
　　Where, O death, is your sting?"
. . . .
But thanks be to God! He gives us the victory through
our Lord Jesus Christ. (1 Corinthians 15:55, 57)

But he said to me, "My grace is sufficient for you, for
my power is made perfect in weakness." Therefore I
will boast all the more gladly about my weaknesses, so
that Christ's power may rest on me. That is why, for
Christ's sake, I delight in weaknesses, in insults, in
hardships, in persecutions, in difficulties. For when I
am weak, then I am strong. (2 Corinthians 12:9-10)

I can do everything through him who gives me strength.
(Philippians 4:13)

Looking Upward

Looking Upward

He *Listens* and *Cares*

"But if it were I, I would appeal to God;
    I would lay my cause before him.
He performs wonders that cannot be fathomed,
    miracles that cannot be counted." (Job 5:8-9)

Cast your cares on the LORD
    and he will sustain you;
    he will never let the righteous fall. (Psalm 55:22)

Hear my cry, O God;
    listen to my prayer.
From the ends of the earth I call to you,
    I call as my heart grows faint;
    lead me to the rock that is higher than I.

                           (Psalm 61:1-2)

He will call upon me, and I will answer him;
    I will be with him in trouble,
    I will deliver him and honor him. (Psalm 91:15)

The LORD is near to all who call on him,
    to all who call on him in truth.
He fulfills the desires of those who fear him;
    he hears their cry and saves them. (Psalm 145:18-19)

The waters closed over my head,
    and I thought I was about to be cut off.
I called on your name, O LORD,
    from the depths of the pit.
You heard my plea: "Do not close your ears
    to my cry for relief."
You came near when I called you,
    and you said, "Do not fear."

Looking Upward

Looking Upward

O Lord, you took up my case;
    you redeemed my life. (Lamentations 3:54-58)

In the same way, the Spirit helps us in our weakness. We do not know what we ought to pray for, but the Spirit himself intercedes for us with groans that words cannot express. And he who searches our hearts knows the mind of the Spirit, because the Spirit intercedes for the saints in accordance with God's will. (Romans 8:26-27)

Cast all your anxiety on him because he cares for you. (1 Peter 5:7)

Timeless *Promises*

"Have I not commanded you? Be strong and courageous. Do not be terrified; do not be discouraged, for the LORD your God will be with you wherever you go." (Joshua 1:9)

I have set the LORD always before me.
    Because he is at my right hand,
    I will not be shaken.
Therefore my heart is glad and my tongue rejoiced;
    my body also will rest secure,
because you will not abandon me to the grave,
    nor will you let your Holy One see decay.
You have made known to me the path of life;
    you will fill me with joy in your presence,
    with eternal pleasures at your right hand.

(Psalm 16:8-11)

And I—in righteousness I will see your face;
    when I awake, I will be satisfied with seeing your
        likeness. (Psalm 17:15)

Looking Upward

Looking *Upward*

My times are in your hands. (Psalm 31:15)

> He will swallow up death forever.
> The Sovereign LORD will wipe away the tears
>   from all faces;
> he will remove the disgrace of his people
>   from all the earth.
>   The LORD has spoken.
> In that day they will say,
> "Surely this is our God;
>   we trusted in him, and he saved us.
> This is the LORD, we trusted in him;
>   let us rejoice and be glad in his salvation."

(Isaiah 25:8-9)

"My sheep listen to my voice; I know them, and they follow me. I give them eternal life, and they shall never perish; no one can snatch them out of my hand." (John 10:27-28)

"Because I live, you also will live." (John 14:19)

"I have told you these things, so that in me you may have peace. In this world you will have trouble. But take heart! I have overcome the world." (John 16:33)

No, in all these things we are more than conquerors through him who loved us. For I am convinced that neither death nor life, neither angels nor demons, neither the present nor the future, nor any powers, neither height nor depth, nor anything else in all creation, will be able to separate us from the love of God that is in Christ Jesus our Lord. (Romans 8:37-39)

Looking Upward

Looking Upward

Rest *for* the *Weary*

The LORD replied, "My Presence will go with you, and I will give you rest." (Exodus 33:14)

There the wicked cease from turmoil,
and there the weary are at rest. (Job 3:17)

I will lie down and sleep in peace,
for you alone, O LORD,
make me dwell in safety. (Psalm 4:8)

When you lie down, you will not be afraid;
when you lie down, your sleep will be sweet.

(Proverbs 3:24)

"Come to me, all you who are weary and burdened, and I will give you rest. Take my yoke upon you and learn from me, for I am gentle and humble in heart, and you will find rest for your souls." (Matthew 11:28-29)

Peace *in* the *Midst* of *Turmoil*

Surely God is my salvation;
I will trust and not be afraid.
The LORD, the LORD, is my strength and my song;
he has become my salvation. (Isaiah 12:2)

You will keep in perfect peace
him whose mind is steadfast,
because he trusts in you. (Isaiah 26:3)

"For I know the plans I have for you," declares the LORD, "plans to prosper you and not to harm you, plans to give you hope and a future. Then you will call

Looking Upward

Looking *Upward*

upon me and come and pray to me, and I will listen to you. You will seek me and find me when you seek me with all your heart." (Jeremiah 29:11-13)

While they were still talking about this, Jesus himself stood among them and said to them, "Peace be with you." (Luke 24:36)

"Peace I leave with you; my peace I give you. I do not give to you as the world gives. Do not let your hearts be troubled and do not be afraid." (John 14:27)

But now in Christ Jesus you who once were far away have been brought near through the blood of Christ. For he himself is our peace. (Ephesians 2:13-14)

Do not be anxious about anything, but in everything, by prayer and petition, with thanksgiving, present your requests to God. And the peace of God, which transcends all understanding, will guard your hearts and your minds in Christ Jesus. (Philippians 4:6-7)

Grace and peace to you from him who is, and who was, and who is to come. (Revelation 1:4)

Looking Upward

Guidance *for* the *Path* Ahead

The LORD himself goes before you and will be with you; he will never leave you nor forsake you. Do not be afraid; do not be discouraged. (Deuteronomy 31:8)

But he knows the way that I take;
when he has tested me, I will come forth as gold.

(Job 23:10)

Looking Upward

If the LORD delights in a man's way,
  he makes his steps firm;
though he stumble, he will not fall,
  for the LORD upholds him with his hand.

(Psalm 37:23-24)

Your word is a lamp to my feet
  and a light for my path. (Psalm 119:105)

I will lead the blind by ways they have not known,
  along unfamiliar paths I will guide them;
I will turn the darkness into light before them
  and make the rough places smooth.
These are the things I will do;
  I will not forsake them. (Isaiah 42:16)

If any of you lacks wisdom, he should ask God, who
gives generously to all without finding fault, and it will
be given to him. (James 1:5)

Our *Eternal* Home

Behold, I will create
  new heavens and a new earth.
The former things will not be remembered,
  nor will they come to mind. (Isaiah 65:17)

"In my Father's house are many rooms; if it were not
so, I would have told you. I am going there to prepare a
place for you. And if I go and prepare a place for you, I
will come back and take you to be with me that you also
may be where I am." (John 14:2-3)

Looking Upward

Looking Upward

Now we know that if the earthly tent we live in is destroyed, we have a building from God, an eternal house in heaven, not built by human hands. (2 Corinthians 5:1)

Therefore we are always confident and know that as long as we are at home in the body we are away from the Lord. We live by faith, not by sight. We are confident, I say, and would prefer to be away from the body and at home with the Lord. (2 Corinthians 5:6-8)

I desire to depart and be with Christ, which is better by far. (Philippians 1:23)

But our citizenship is in heaven. And we eagerly await a Savior from there, the Lord Jesus Christ, who, by the power that enables him to bring everything under his control, will transform our lowly bodies so that they will be like his glorious body. (Philippians 3:20-21)

Brothers, we do not want you to be ignorant about those who fall asleep, or to grieve like the rest of men, who have no hope. We believe that Jesus died and rose again and so we believe that God will bring with Jesus those who have fallen asleep in him. (1 Thessalonians 4:13-14)

For the Lord himself will come down from heaven, with a loud command, with the voice of the archangel and with the trumpet call of God, and the dead in Christ will rise first. After that, we who are still alive and are left will be caught up together with them in the clouds to meet the Lord in the air. And so we will be with the Lord forever. (1 Thessalonians 4:16-17)

For I am already being poured out like a drink offering, and the time has come for my departure. I have fought

Looking Upward

Looking Upward

the good fight, I have finished the race, I have kept the faith. Now there is in store for me the crown of righteousness, which the Lord, the righteous Judge, will award to me on that day—and not only to me, but also to all who have longed for his appearing. (2 Timothy 4:6-8)

We wait for the blessed hope—the glorious appearing of our great God and Savior, Jesus Christ. (Titus 2:13)

So do not throw away your confidence; it will be richly rewarded. You need to persevere so that when you have done the will of God, you will receive what he has promised. For in just a very little while, "He who is coming will come and will not delay." (Hebrews 10:35-37)

For here we do not have an enduring city, but we are looking for the city that is to come. (Hebrews 13:14)

Praise be to the God and Father of our Lord Jesus Christ! In his great mercy he has given us new birth into a living hope through the resurrection of Jesus Christ from the dead, and into an inheritance that can never perish, spoil or fade—kept in heaven for you. (1 Peter 1:3-4)

But in keeping with his promise we are looking forward to a new heaven and a new earth, the home of righteousness. (2 Peter 3:13)

After this I looked and there before me was a great multitude that no one could count, from every nation, tribe, people and language, standing before the throne and in front of the Lamb. They were wearing white robes and were holding palm branches in their hands. And they cried out in a loud voice:

Looking Upward

Looking Upward

"Salvation belongs to our God,
who sits on the throne,
and to the Lamb."

All the angels were standing around the throne and around the elders and the four living creatures. They fell down on their faces before the throne and worshiped God, saying:

"Amen!
Praise and glory
and wisdom and thanks and honor
and power and strength
be to our God for ever and ever.
Amen!" (Revelation 7:9-12)

I answered, "Sir, you know."

And he said, "These are they who have come out of the great tribulation; they have washed their robes and made them white in the blood of the Lamb. Therefore,

"they are before the throne of God
and serve him day and night in his temple;
and he who sits on the throne will spread
his tent over them.
Never again will they hunger;
never again will they thirst.
The sun will not beat upon them,
nor any scorching heat.
For the Lamb at the center of the throne will be
their shepherd;
he will lead them to springs of living water.
And God will wipe away every tear from
their eyes." (Revelation 7:14-17)

Then I saw a new heaven and a new earth, for the first heaven and the first earth had passed away, and there was no longer any sea. I saw the Holy City, the new Je-

Looking *Upward*

rusalem, coming down out of heaven from God, prepared as a bride beautifully dressed for her husband. And I heard a loud voice from the throne saying, "Now the dwelling of God is with men, and he will live with them. They will be his people, and God himself will be with them and be their God. He will wipe every tear from their eyes. There will be no more death or mourning or crying or pain, for the old order of things has passed away." (Revelation 21:1-4)

. . . and there we will never again say good-bye.

Looking Upward

Looking *Upward*

Sample *Obituaries*

Writing the obituary of your loved one can be very difficult. Emotions well up and tears blur your vision as you agonize over how to write it all in such a tiny space. It helps to know that there is no one right way to complete this task.

Look in your local newspaper to get an idea of how most are being done. Some papers will print the basic information free of charge. These are very brief and usually come under the section entitled "Funeral Notices" or "Death Notices." Some will allow you to word it as you wish, and others require a standard format. Think through what you want to say and how you want it worded before you call. Some will take the information over the phone, and others will request a fax.

Funeral *or* Death *Notices*

Example #1:

> Thomas Seth Wilson. Memorial service will be held Saturday, October 6, 2003, at 2:00 p.m. at Rolling Hills Church, 2445 Wygant Avenue in Portland, Oregon. Reception following at church.

Example #2:

> Linda S. Rhodes, loving mother of Jared and Cynthia. Viewing will be held Sunday, May 19, 2004, from 12-2 p.m. Funeral service Monday, May 20 at 1 p.m. with reception following at Rose City Funeral Home, 8876 SW Hillside Dr. in Portland, Oregon. (503) 555-3298.

Obituaries

Obituaries are usually quite a bit longer, with prices corresponding to length. Include information pertinent to the funeral services, a summary of your loved one's life and its highlights (making note of special interests and achievements), surviving relatives (usually just immediate family) and where contributions may be sent.

Example:

Olive G. Sanders

Funeral services for Olive G. Sanders will be held at 10:00 a.m. on Wednesday, February 3, 2003, at Damascus Christian Church, 89 Sempre Rd. in Damascus, Oregon. Burial will follow at Mt. Scott Cemetery. Mrs. Sanders died in her home in Marysville on January 28, 2003. She was seventy-two years of age.

Olive was born in Wadegrads, Indiana, on September 14, 1930. Her parents were James and Frances Baker. After graduating from high school, she was employed as a live-in housekeeper and nanny. On August 8, 1955, she married Abraham Sanders in Upland, Georgia. She raised three children. She loved cooking and working in her garden and raising flowers. She was very active in the Porterville Lutheran Church.

She is survived by sons James A. and Jan Sanders of Vancouver, Washington, Carl F. Sanders of Portland, Oregon, and daughter Lynnette and Steven Johnston of Boise, Idaho, a brother Paul N. Hatcher of Los Altos, California, and six grandchildren.

Contributions in her memory may be made to the Porterville Missionary Fund.

Marysville Funeral chapel is in charge of arrangements (503) 555-0926.

Sample *Funeral* Service

A variety of factors help determine what you incorporate into your unique service: where it is held (funeral home, graveside, church, home, etc.), personality and personal wishes of the deceased, faith of the deceased and/or that of the living relatives, desired length of service and many more.

There is not just one right way to put it all together. See "Planning the Service" in Part One for a list of things to do and thoughts to consider. The following is a copy of what our family gave each guest at my father's memorial service.

Front Cover:
Photo of Dad

Inside Left Page:

In Honor of the Homegoing of
Robert O'Brien

Born—December 3, 1925
With His Lord—July 29, 2001

Service held at
Rolling Hills Community Church
Danville, California

Pastor Roger Martin, Officiating

<u>*Scripture*</u>
"For our citizenship is in heaven, from which
also we eagerly wait for a Savior,
the Lord Jesus Christ."
(Philippians 3:20, NASB)

Inside Right Page:

Special Music .... Tom Lucia/Kathryn Lucia
"The Lord's Prayer"

Welcome and Prayer .... Pastor Martin

Congregational Song .... "Amazing Grace"

Looking Back .... Pastor Martin/Welby O'Brien

Special Music .... Tom Lucia/Kathryn Lucia
"Because He Lives"

Looking Forward .... Pastor Martin

Congregational Song .... "How Great Thou Art"

Prayer .... Pastor Martin

* Guests are invited to stay for lunch following the service.

* Notes to the family are available in the narthex for you
to express your memories, thoughts and love.

Back Cover:

A Final Word from Bob

*Bob's personal faith in Jesus Christ as his Savior
was of utmost importance to him. It would be his desire
that every friend and acquaintance have the same
personal faith that he had. He would be
so honored if you would read the enclosed article
written by his daughter, Welby.
[See Appendix E: "The Lifeboat."]
The end of the article explains how each person can establish
a personal relationship with Jesus Christ
as their Savior and Lord.*

Helping *Children* Grieve

ny child who is old enough to love is old enough to grieve, so we must never underestimate the grief work of children. It simply is not possible to protect them from loss experiences. Children are not short adults, and they grieve in ways unique to children. It is our job, as caring adults, to respond in ways that allow them to feel supported.

Supporting *Children* at *School*

Educators who don't preplan ways of supporting children *before* a death occurs will find themselves pressured and less able to intervene in helpful ways during the crisis.

Telling the Child at School

The child should be told by a trusted authority in a private, quiet place. Ask someone who is known to the child to remain with the child after he or she is told. Give the information directly and simply, including who died and how the death occurred. Don't over-talk. Be honest. Tell the child what will happen next. Invite questions. Tell the child you will help him and that you know this is a scary, hard experience.

Telling Other Children

Prior to informing the other children of the death, send a brief reminder to teachers regarding methods of supporting children. Inform the student body in an assembly. Invite all personnel who had contact with the student (cafeteria workers, bus drivers, etc, if possible). Give factual information about the death; describe common reactions to grief, so children understand what is normal; and invite children to talk with the school counselor or to participate in a small group if they would like to do this. Give the children permission to continue their daily routine. Tell them it is OK to have fun. Invite children to attend the funeral when this information is known and excuse them from school to do so.

Provide a brief information sheet (see end of article) for students to take home to parents that provides guidelines for supporting children. Tell parents that it is helpful for a grieving child to come to school as soon as the child feels ready.

If the death involves a staff member, teacher or another student, it is helpful to invite students to respond to the family of the person who died by writing letters ("What I Liked Most About Mr. Brown," etc); make an art project together or participate in the funeral with the band or choral group, if invited.

During the Weeks That Follow the Death

During class time, schedule time to share memories of the student who died. If students were not able to attend the funeral, plan a memorial service at school, which could include singing a love song while lighting candles, releasing balloons outside and a brief talk about heaven. For several weeks leave empty the desk or chair where the child who died sat. Establish a memorial by planting a tree on the school grounds or making some permanent art project. Expect unpredictable relapses, "grief attacks," which are triggered by various events throughout the school year. This resurging grief is often present for many years in children.

It isn't possible for children to finish their grief work until they know the extent of their loss, so the work of mourning is often a long process. Our task is to help children move toward their grief, not away from it. The goal of good grief work is not that the child gets "over it," but that the child *grows* from the experience.

NOTE: The previous material was authored by Doris Sanford, Heart to Heart Inc., 16332 SE Heart Place, Milwaukie, OR 97267. (503) 654-2029. E-mail: dorissanford@webtv.net

Doris Sanford and Graci Evans, her illustrator and friend, have written twenty-nine children's books published by Multnomah Press and other publishers which deal in realistic yet simple terms with death, divorce, self esteem, sexual abuse, parental alcoholism and sibling drug use. Mrs. Sanford is an RN and has a master's degree in clinical psychology.

The handout for staff and parents appears on the next few pages.

Supporting Grieving
Children at Home

Do's

1. Tell the truth ("I don't know" is an OK answer to "why" questions).

2. Maintain structure, rules, limits. It provides security.

3. Touch, hold, hug.

4. Save special items from the deceased person to give the child later (a collection, a Bible, a sweatshirt, etc.).

5. Share your faith. ("God knows what has happened to us. He loves us and will help us.")

6. Be a good role model. Cry in front of the child. ("I miss Grandma.")

7. Talk about loss and death before a significant death occurs, if possible. Visit a cemetery, use nature (i.e., a dead bird) for discussion.

8. Give the child a choice about going to the funeral. If he is under eight years old, bring along an adult who can leave with him or her at any time.

9. Tell the child he did not cause the death by his angry thoughts.

10. Tell the child who will take care of him if you die.

11. Recognize that children express grief physically. They "flush out the wound" by beating, pounding, running it out.

12. Allow children to select the play activities they need to work through their grief.

13. Talk about heaven. Use Scripture to describe it.

14. Let the child "talk" about his feelings through drawings.

15. Give the child something to do. It will combat his helplessness. For example: Plant a memory tree, write a story, take flowers to the grave.

16. Read children's books which deal with loss so the child knows his feelings are normal.

17. Use third-person language in talking to children. It is less threatening to say, "Many children feel . . ." instead of "Do you feel . . .?"

18. Look through photo albums at pictures of the deceased with the child.

19. Talk about the loss whenever the child brings up the subject.

20. Answer only what is asked. Let the child be in charge of what he is ready to hear.

21. Expect children to regress somewhat, i.e., to cling, be afraid. Rocking and night lights are fine.

22. Tell the child the exact cause of death. ("Grandma's heart wouldn't work anymore.")

Don'ts

1. Don't underestimate the child's grief.

2. Don't try to protect the child from feelings of pain and loss.

3. Don't assume the child will respond to the loss as you have.

4. Don't worry about saying the "right words." You can't hide feelings from children, no matter what you say.

5. Don't find something "good" about death, i.e., "Aren't you glad Mommy doesn't hurt anymore?" "Isn't it wonderful that God's love was shared at the funeral?"

6. Don't associate tears with grief. Some children cry, some don't. Both may be equally affected.

7. Don't push the child to "talk about it." A child will tell us how he feels in the way he is able, which is usually through his behavior.

8. Don't be afraid of losing control or crying in front of the child. Tears give the child permission to be real too.

9. Don't shut the child out by sending him to a babysitter. Include him in the family sadness.

10. Don't be overly simplistic about death, i.e., put all the focus on heaven and none on the feelings of loss.

11. Don't replace a dead pet immediately. Let the child grieve.

12. Don't say, "Now you're the man of the house."

13. Don't allow the child to assume the role of emotional caregiver to the parents.

14. Don't worry about the child's poor appetite. Give plenty of drinks.

15. Don't tell the child he will feel better in time. "Time heals all wounds" is a lie. Some wounds get infected.

16. Don't use abstract language to "soften" death. Children are concrete thinkers. Instead of saying, "Grandpa passed away," say, "Grandpa died."

17. Don't promise *you* won't die. You can say, "I think I will live until I'm very, very old, but no one knows for sure."

18. Don't be afraid to initiate talking about death. Mention the person's name who died, i.e., "I know Grandpa died and I'm sure you miss him very much."

19. Don't assume a child will always want to talk about the death. Children can only handle "bits and pieces" of grief at a time.

20. In a church or school setting, don't single out a grieving child for special privileges. He needs to feel he is treated the same as his peers.

Preparing *for* Your *Own* Good-bye

After my father died, it took us a while to gather together all the important papers, documents and information. One day we came across a workbook in his desk entitled *Important Things I Want My Family to Know*. We opened it eagerly, only to chuckle. It was totally blank. He had good intentions, I'm sure, but he never executed them. If he had completed the booklet, he would have made our job much easier.

The following is a checklist of things to consider putting in order for the sake of your own loved ones.

___ Collect and organize all pertinent information: will or trust, bank accounts, safe deposit box, investments, insurance (health, life, car, home, etc.), Social Security, mortgage, deed, car title and registration, veteran's information, funeral home arrangements, memorial service wishes and anything else you want to include.

___ Be sure your will is legal and up-to-date.

___ Put all your important information together in an obvious or agreed-upon place. Communicate with your loved ones where they can find it.

___ Pay your debts.

___ Consider being a donor, either organ and tissue or whole body. In most cases, donation does not affect the timing of the funeral. When the whole body is donated to medical research, there will be certain charges, such as a transportation fee, and perhaps others depending on your choice of services. You can sign and carry a Uniform Donor Card in your wallet (must have signatures of two witnesses). Check with your state's motor vehicle department to see if you can also have a "D" noted on your driver's license.

___ Examine the options for prepaid funeral home services. It allows you to make the arrangements at current prices.

___ Write out what you want in your service.

___ Clear out clutter. Go through drawers, closets, garage, etc. and get rid of everything you don't need.

___ Attend to any rifts with family or friends. Let your loved ones know how much you love them every day.

___ Be at peace with God. (See Appendix E: "Message of Hope: The Lifeboat.")

Message *of* Hope: *The* Lifeboat

Imagine for a moment that you were born and raised on the *Titanic*. You never had a choice as to your condition and destiny—that's just the way you began your existence in the universe. Having grown up quickly, you didn't mind this lifestyle. In fact, it was promising to be quite pleasurable.

You'd been taught that life has its ups and downs, its seasick moments, disappointments at the dinner table and on the dance floor. In fact, some people were angry at the captain, whom they'd never seen, questioning how he could allow pain and still claim to be a loving captain.

You'd also been taught the importance of being a good person in order to win the captain's favor and hopefully ensure a pleasant future.

Can *You* Trust *the* Ship?

You admired the beauty of the ship and reveled in its ability to provide you with the comforts of life you felt you deserved. You rested securely as you pondered the ship's strength. Alone with your thoughts, you were troubled momentarily by fleeting fear, which was quickly allayed as you drew comfort from what you saw around you. The truth was so evident—how could you have questioned it? Chiding yourself for your moment of weakness, you reminded yourself that you could trust this ship—the ship you had grown to know and love, the ship that everyone knew was so solid and inde-structible that there would never be a need for lifeboats.

Caught up in your immediate surroundings and the voyage itself, you neglected to notice the majesty of the roaring sea and the splendor of the star-studded sky at night. Who was responsible for all of that? Had you considered your final des-tination?

But why bother about those things? You were having a wonderful time in the present. There would be plenty of opportunities later to consider your destination.

Suddenly you were jolted awake by clamor and confusion. The ship was sinking. It was going down fast. Terrified, you cried, "Help! Help me!"

No one could help. They were going down too. The ship had failed you. All of your good deeds meant nothing for you now.

"Good news!" someone shouted. "It is finished! Every-one can now be saved!"

You learned that the captain himself had plunged into the black, icy water to release a giant lifeboat that floated to the sur-face. They said that even before the ship was built the captain knew what he would have to do to provide the lifeboat. You watched as the captain's body floated off into the darkness.

Freedom *to* Board

They said that the captain would never force anyone to get on the lifeboat, but that he wanted the people to have the free-dom to board willingly. Amid the panic and confusion as the ship began to submerge, you observed this freedom of choice.

Some argued that it was pretty narrow to claim there was only one lifeboat. Others clung to the ship, refusing to let go of their source of life and pleasure. Some sadly insisted that they weren't good enough to get into the lifeboat.

Others were indignant at the thought of boarding a lifeboat with imperfect people, hypocrites and the politically incorrect. Realizing they had only minutes to live, some rushed to the dining room to eat all they could.

Politely, some granted you the right to believe in the lifeboat as long as you respected their right to believe differently. Others preferred to stick with their friends and family who had chosen to stay on the ship.

There were some who said the captain never died to provide a lifeboat. It was all just a feel-good fairy tale giving everyone false hopes.

Others were holding debates to prove that there never *was* a captain.

Some refused to listen, explaining that they knew all there was to know about lifeboats since they had gone to lifeboat class every Sunday. A few declined, complaining that they once tried to read the Lifeboat Instruction Manual but didn't understand it.

A few of the younger people weren't worried, since their parents were already aboard the lifeboat. Therefore, they too would be OK. Some said the captain was a good man but that he certainly was not capable of providing a lifeboat. Others boasted that they didn't need a lifeboat as they began to swim to shore.

Some expressed offense at the scare tactics, getting people all upset when there wasn't a problem. The ship was fine, they claimed. Still others argued cynically that the lifeboat was just a moneymaking scheme.

Talk of other lifeboat options distracted many from boarding the real lifeboat. Some were determined to complain about the captain for allowing discomfort and refused to accept that he really cared.

Calmly, others said that there was still plenty of time. They would get into the lifeboat after they had had a chance to live their lives. Some challenged the belief that a safe shore even existed, since, like the captain, the shore could not be seen.

Still others complained that the lifeboat was all they ever heard about, and they wished certain people would quit shoving lifeboat information down their throats.

And a few reached out and climbed to safety in the lifeboat.

What would you do? Now is a good time to decide. The captain is waiting on the shore for you with open arms.

Secure *Your* Place *in* the *Lifeboat*

How do we secure our places in the lifeboat? Salvation, our lifeboat, comes only through Christ's death—the death of the Captain who rose again and is now waiting for us. Here are the steps to securing your salvation.

1. Acknowledge your helplessness as a sinner before God. "For all have sinned and fall short of the glory of God" (Romans 3:23).

2. Believe that God loves you and Christ died for *you*. "But God demonstrates his own love for us in this: While we were still sinners, Christ died for us" (Romans 5:8).

3. Honestly admit to God that you need Him. "For, 'Everyone who calls on the name of the Lord will be saved' " (Romans 10:13).

4. Choose God's free gift of eternal life only through His Son. "For the wages of sin is death, but the gift of God is eternal life in Christ Jesus our Lord" (Romans 6:23).

5. Trust Him to carry you safely to shore. "He who has the Son has life; he who does not have the Son of God does not have life. I write these things to you who believe in the name of the Son of God so that you may know that you have eternal life" (1 John 5:12-13).

From Alliance Life *magazine, June 9, 1999, pp. 8-10. Used by permission.*